NOW THAT THE
FUNERAL
IS OVER
THE COMMON SENSE
GUIDE FOR GRIEVING PEOPLE

www.wilkinsonpublishing.com.au

Published by:
Wilkinson Publishing Pty Ltd
ACN 006 042 173
Level 4, 2 Collins Street
Melbourne, Vic 3000
Ph: 03 9654 5446
www.wilkinsonpublishing.com.au

The CiP for this title is available through the National Library of Australia.

Design: Lee Walker

ABOUT THE AUTHOR

Doris Zagdanski has had the opportunity to meet hundreds of grieving people. She has volunteered her time as a Home Visitor to families in Victoria whose child died unexpectedly from Sudden Infant Death Syndrome and is well known to many support groups for the bereaved. She has worked on the front line as a funeral director and is still employed in the funeral industry.

For the past 30 years, her career has centred on grief education throughout Australia and overseas.

She is the author of seven books on loss, grief and empathy and is a sought after conference speaker and trainer in her field – her message about grief is contemporary, educational, entertaining and real.

CONTENTS

CHAPTER 1

WHAT YOU SHOULD KNOW ABOUT GRIEF

There is no easy way around grief. It is a natural response to the loss of someone special or something we value. Grief is not well understood in our society and some people try to deny it, postpone it or dodge it.

However, when someone close to you has died, there will be big and small adjustments which have to be made in your life — and these could bring uncertainty, frustration, fear, sadness and change as each new day comes along. You will change. Your routine will change. Your moods will change. All of this is called 'grief'. It's really about adapting to changes in your life, your thoughts, your hopes, your beliefs and your future.

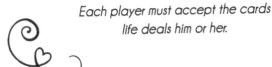

Each player must accept the cards life deals him or her.

Voltaire

There is no set pattern to follow when you are grieving. Even members of the one family, who are mourning the loss of the same person, will show their grief in diverse ways. Why does this happen? Because there are specific factors which affect the grief of individuals differently. These include:

YOUR PERSONALITY

How you cope with stress: do you communicate your feelings easily to others or do you clam up? Do you keep really busy to avoid thinking about your problems? Do you believe you must be strong or always in control? Do you worry about the opinion of others, especially if you become upset?

THE CONNECTION

What was unique about your relationship with the person who died? What were the positives and the negatives? How strong was the connection – there can be a very close bond between a mother and a newborn baby even though they may not have 'known' each other for long. The loss of this relationship is just as important as the loss of a marriage of many years. The same is true for same sex relationships, lovers, best friends – anyone who means something to you.

*A thousand mile journey
begins with one step.*

Lao Tse

CIRCUMSTANCES OF THE DEATH

Was it sudden, untimely? Was the person too young? How was the news broken? Was there time to say goodbye? Did you see the person after death? Did you go to the funeral? Even when the death is expected, on the day it happens, you can find yourself in shock and unprepared. Sometimes when people did not say an adequate goodbye, they can deny the death or act as if the person has just gone away for a time. When death is sudden, you can be left with 'unfinished business' and regret the things you didn't say or do, or wish you could have done more.

SUPPORT

Do you have sensitive people to rely on for support such as family, church, colleagues, a doctor or employer? Do your friends allow you to show your feelings or do they expect you to get on with living now that the funeral is over? Remember that sometimes males receive little support because the people around them believe they are strong and can cope on their own. Some men also believe they should not show their feelings to others so they do not talk about their grief. This can be difficult when a partner or friend wants to talk about what's happened and find they get nowhere in the conversation.

Here is something to think about – support is not measured by the number of people you know or how large your family is. Helpful support comes from people who let you do your grieving and stay around for the long haul.

Life is not the way it is supposed to be.
It's the way it is. The way you cope with it is
what makes the difference.

Virginia Satir

OVERLOAD OF PROBLEMS

Has this death come at a time when you have other problems to deal with? You could feel swamped by an overload of feelings or not know which way to turn. Problems such as financial worries, family conflict or poor health can impact on you now. Or maybe there is a loss somewhere in the past, even from your childhood, that has been swept under the carpet and may therefore make your present grief more complex and difficult to resolve.

Can you see why it is important to recognise each person's grief as a unique experience? When you do this, you will find it easier to understand how you and the rest of your family, and even your friends, are coping.

The melody that the loved one played upon the piano of your life will never be played quite that way again, but we must not close the keyboard and allow the instrument to gather dust. We must seek out other artists of the spirit, new friends who gradually will help us to find the road to life again, who will walk that road with us.

Joshua Loth Liebman

Grief is also for children. Like adults, children will react to the news of death individually, perhaps with unexpected responses. The child may say it's not true or lash out physically or verbally. Wanting to be left alone or being curious and full of questions may be more common for some children than sadness. Fears may surface — Who's going to look after us now? Will we have to move house? I'm afraid to go to sleep. I don't understand what's going on.

Children are best helped by adults who give them clear and honest explanations about death and who allow tears or other feelings to surface without criticism or rejection. To say to a young child: "We lost Grandma in the night" or "Daddy has gone to heaven" can be vague and confusing. Such explanations equate death with simply going away and can leave the child with the expectation that at some future time the person will return.

Young children may become clingy, afraid of the dark, and regress to bed wetting or thumb sucking.

Regular routines like meal times and bed time stories, cuddles, hugs and some quiet time together will help a child who is feeling frightened or unsure about the changes happening in the family.

Not only am I going to experience fear whenever I'm on unfamiliar territory, but so is everyone else.

Susan Jeffers

Teenagers can be particularly vulnerable when a school friend or family member dies because their grief may become complicated by the usual ups and downs associated with adolescence. Their need to appear 'grown up' in front of their peers, or their family, could result in isolation and difficulty in asking for help or expressing feelings.

Sometimes teens show their sadness, anger or confusion through their behaviour – withdrawal from their usual activities, disinterest in school, aggressive outbursts, risk taking behaviour, mood swings … just to name a few.

Teens are helped when we listen to them, take their feelings seriously, and show that we understand why they are out of sorts and upset. To say their feelings are silly or to criticise their concerns sends a message of rejection and may create further isolation and anxiety. They may try drugs and alcohol to block out the pain, rather than ask for help.

It is not necessary for adults to hide their own tears from children of any age – your grief will show them that they need not be ashamed or scared to express their own. By doing this, they will not carry unresolved childhood losses into their adult lives, nor will they learn unhelpful ways of coping with grief such as masking their true feelings or believing that they must bear their hurt, uncertainty, questions, anger or fear silently.

Everything that happens to you is your teacher.
The secret is to learn to sit at the feet of your own life
and be taught by it.

Polly Berrien Berends

Grief hurts – few would argue with that. Throughout history, artists have captured their pain on canvas, composers have used the instruments of the orchestra to convey their emotions and writers have allowed their pens to spill their thoughts onto paper.

Our grief needs to be expressed. Our feelings need to be acknowledged. The reality of separation and loss needs to be accepted. We need to find helpful ways to get our feelings 'off our chest' so that they don't get stuck inside.

Once the numbness of tragedy has worn off, we need to work through the tasks of reorganisation and readjustment – as unwelcome as they may be. It's about adapting to new routines, learning new skills to manage day to day living, finding ways to deal with the empty space that's been left behind and the conversations that can't be had. This is what we call our 'grief work'. It is through this work that we rebuild our lives and find meaning again in living.

There is always another chance ... This thing we call 'failure' is not the falling down, but the staying down.

Mary Pickford

CHAPTER 2

GRIEF REACTIONS
AND BEHAVIOURS

There are many interpretations of the way grief affects people. Whether it is described as a process of phases or steps or stages, one thing is certain. You must be prepared for a variety of reactions and feelings, some which may be more intense than you ever expected and others which won't affect you at all.

Grief is likely to influence you on four different levels – emotionally, behaviourally, physically and intellectually. In other words, it may affect the way you feel, it may challenge your beliefs, it may weaken your health and it may cause you to question your values and reassess your lifestyle. You might do and say things that are out of character, you may act in ways that are unexpected. That's what happens when you're grieving.

Here are some possible behaviours, feelings and reactions which are commonly considered as 'normal grief'. Remember there is no set order to 'feel' these in; the list is only useful as a guide to establish that grief like this is not unusual.

Those things that hurt instruct.

Benjamin Franklin

SHOCK DISBELIEF & NUMBNESS

My mind can't take it all in.

My body seems to be on "auto pilot".

I don't want to believe it's true.

How could this have happened – it's so sudden!

It can't be true, I only saw him yesterday.

ANGER

It's not fair.

I hate God.

Why did this happen to our family?

How could you leave me and the kids?

Why couldn't the doctors do something to save you?

*Do what you can, with what you have,
where you are.*

Theodore Roosevelt

DEPRESSION

I don't care any more.

Why bother getting up in the morning?

I'll never get over this.

I wish I were dead too.

Without you nothing matters to me.

PANIC

How will I cope on my own?

Who's going to pay the bills?

What if I drop my bundle?

What if something happens to me – who'll take
care of the kids?

I depended on you for everything – I don't know what
to do, where to start.

People cry, not because they are weak.
It's because they've been strong for too long.

Unknown

REJECTION

How could he do this to me, leaving me all on my own?

Where is God now?

Where are all those friends who said they'd do
anything to help?

Why couldn't you tell us you needed help?

Why didn't you fight harder to live?

PREOCCUPATION

I can't get my mind off this.

I keep going over and over what happened.

I just can't think about anything else ...
nothing else matters.

My mind keeps wandering, even when I'm at work.

Everywhere I look reminds me of you.

Be careful how you think.
Your life is shaped by your thoughts.

Proverbs

AGGRESSION

I feel like smashing, bashing, swearing, yelling,
and thumping my fists.

I want to lash out at something, someone, the world.

Don't preach to me about God's will!

How would you know how I'm feeling!

How dare you tell me I should be over it by now!

GUILT & REGRETS

I just wish we hadn't had that argument.

If only I'd gone into his room earlier – maybe I
could have done something.

If I could just turn back the clock.

I never got a chance to say I loved him.

Why didn't I listen when he said he was so depressed?

*My favourite thing is to go
where I've never been.*

Diane Arbus

SADNESS

I miss her so much.

I feel so empty inside.

Will I ever smile again?

I just can't stop crying.

It's so sad, she had so much to live for.

INDIFFERENCE

I don't give a damn about anything any more.

I can't be bothered hearing about everyone's problems,
I've got enough of my own.

What's the point of going on?

I don't care about anything these days,
it seems so pointless.

I just can't get myself motivated.

*It is good to have an end to journey towards; but it is the
journey that matters in the end.*

Ursula K. Guin

FEAR

I'm frightened to be on my own.

I'm scared I'll forget what you looked like.

Night time is really scary now.

I can't imagine a future without you – what if I can't cope?

We did everything together – how will I
survive on my own?

IDEALISATION

He was the best husband you could have wished for.

We never, ever had an argument.

She was the most perfect person in the world.

He was a real saint.

I'll never meet anyone like him again.

*Courage is resistance to fear,
not absence of it.*

Mark Twain

FEELING SICK

There's a great big knot in my stomach.

My head's thumping and I'm aching all over.

I'm feeling so tense in my muscles.

I just can't be bothered eating – I feel like
I'm going to be sick.

I seem to pick up every virus that's going around.

CONFUSION

I can't think straight.

I keep forgetting things.

I can't make decisions.

I feel all mixed up.

One minute I'm okay and then all of a sudden

*Don't be afraid to go out on a limb.
That's where the fruit is.*

Arthur Lenehan

LONELINESS

The house just feels so empty.

I miss all the little things we did together.

I don't seem to fit in with my friends any more.

There's no one to talk to, no one understands me.

Even in a room full of people I feel like a
complete stranger.

CRYING

Should the children see me crying?

I just can't cry.

I can't go past the hospital without crying.

When I see other babies I just start to cry.

Will I ever stop crying?

Never give in. Never give in. Never give in.

Sir Winston Churchill

INSOMNIA & DREAMS

I lie awake all night ... thinking.

I'm too scared to go to bed at night.

I keep having dreams about what happened.

She talks to me in my dreams.

Why are the nights so long and lonely?

BITTERNESS, RESENTMENT & JEALOUSY

Why my husband? He never hurt anyone in his life.

It's not fair – God's taken my only child.

Someone's got to pay for this. I want to get even!

I'm so envious of other families who never have anything go wrong.

I can't stand seeing happy couples together.

*To dream of the person you would like to be,
is to waste the person you are.*

Unknown

LOW ENERGY

I just don't feel like going out or playing sport – I'm too tired.

I can't be bothered with the kids, they just get on my nerves.

Life's a drag.

It's an effort just to get out of bed.

I feel so drained.

DENIAL

I don't want to hear about it.

It's not true, it's not true.

I hate the cemetery, I don't want to go there.

I've told myself he's just gone away for a holiday.

Don't talk to me about it – I'm trying to forget.

The fact that something has happened to a million other people diminishes neither grief nor joy.

Unknown

WITHDRAWAL

I want to shut myself away.

Why don't you just leave me alone!

I want to run away and come back when this is all over.

I'll have another drink, then I won't think about it.

What's the point in going out – it's no fun on my own.

VOICES & VISIONS

I can hear him calling for me.

I'm sure I saw him in a crowd.

I can feel his presence in the house.

It's like she's still with me.

I thought I saw him in the distance.

I will go anywhere, as long as it's forward.

David Livingston

FRUSTRATION

It's all getting on top of me.

When am I going to feel better?

Why don't people understand me?

I hate feeling like this.

Nothing's the same anymore.

RELIEF

I'm glad all the suffering is finally over.

I don't know if I could have taken much more.

He's with God now.

I'm glad I saw him – he looked so peaceful.

Now we can start to pick up the pieces and get
on with our life.

*God gives us the music.
We are our own instruments.*

Flavia Weedn

KEEPING BUSY

I've got to keep my mind off this.

I can't sit still for one minute.

If I keep myself busy then I won't stop to
think about it.

He wouldn't want me to be moping around.

I can't drop my bundle – they're all depending on me.

GOING CRAZY

I've never felt like this before.

I'm so mixed up I must be going mad.

I used to be so calm about everything and now
I just don't know where I'm heading.

What's the matter with me? I used to be so strong.

Are my feelings normal?

What the caterpillar calls the end the world,
the master calls the butterfly.

Richard Bach

QUESTIONING

Why me? Why him? Why her?
Why not someone else?

Why did God let this happen?

Why wasn't there a cure for this?

Why weren't our prayers answered?

Why so young? Why? Why? Why?

EMPTINESS

I feel like something is always missing.

A part of me has died.

My arms just ache to hold my child again.

I feel like I'm just going through the motions of living.

There's such a huge gap in my life now.

There are two times in your life when you'll always be right. When you say "I can", and when you say, "I can't".

Unknown

LONGING & PINING

I just want things to be the way they were.

If I could just hold you in my arms again.

All I can think about is how things were
when we were together.

I want you back!

Not a minute goes by that you're not on my mind.

ADJUSTMENT

I'm looking forward to …

I have more good days than bad ones now. That knot
in my stomach has gone.

I seem to spend less time thinking about the past.

I can look back at what happened and it doesn't get to
me like it used to.

Why me? I guess I've learned that these things
don't just happen to other people – they happen to ordinary
people like me too.

It hasn't been easy but I know I can survive this.

*When you are sorrowful, look again in your heart,
and you shall see that in truth you are weeping for
that which has been your delight.*

Kahlil Gibran

Here is one way we can see some evidence of adjustment:

"It's a mixture of being alone and cold and lost. It's a heavy feeling – you're tired, no energy, you just drag yourself along ..."

Janet, aged 15, after her school friend died.

"I've been thinking about it. It's starting to make sense. It's become clearer. I'm more at ease with my feelings, I can understand them better."

Janet, 12 months later.

Our lives are shaped as much by those who leave us as they are by those who stay. Loss is our legacy. Insight is our gift. Memory is our guide.

Hope Edelman

It might seem unbelievable now, but most people learn to readjust to their loss. You can do this too. This doesn't mean that your grief will be 'cured' or that you should forget the person who has died. Even in years to come there might be occasions when you will still feel sad. There will always be reminders and memory triggers that could make you emotional. There will always be family occasions when someone special is missing.

What is probably the difference, when you have moved through your grief, is that the loss is not the total preoccupation of your thoughts. Your energy for living will return. There will be no need to put on a happy face to please others – you will be able to smile again because you really want to. Life will be different, but that doesn't mean you can't appreciate it again. You won't feel guilty for laughing.

It is best not to put a time frame on the whole experience of grief. This creates unrealistic expectations and doesn't allow for individual differences. However, this may not stop the people around you urging you to 'put it behind you and get on with your life'. This is often easier said than done. You will get through your grief in your own good time not when others tell you that you should be over it. Their discomfort and difficulty in understanding your grief says much more about them than it does about you.

I don't think of all the misery,
but of all the beauty that remains.

Anne Frank

Those who try to walk around the edge of their grief do themselves no favours. By avoiding the suffering, they in fact avoid the potential for growth that is concealed beneath every crisis.

It's interesting to note that the word 'crisis' comes from the Latin 'krinein' which has a number of interpretations – *turning point, crossroad, hour of decision.*

When we are grieving, it is up to us to choose whether we will be defeated by our loss or whether we will try to survive it. This idea may sound impossible especially when our grief is fresh and our feelings are raw. But, in reality, we always have choices and sometimes it's only a choice of attitude.

When a man finds that it is his destiny to suffer, he will have to accept his suffering as his task; his single and unique task. He will have to acknowledge the fact that even in his suffering he is unique and alone in the universe. No one can relieve him on his suffering or suffer in his place. His unique opportunity lies in the way in which he bears his burden.

Viktor Frankl

CHAPTER 3

HELPING YOURSELF
TO READJUST

Some grieving people will wait for time to heal their sorrow. But this doesn't get them very far. You will need to deal with your feelings and face the changes in your life – there's just no easy way out of it.

In his book, *Go Gently*, David Morawetz describes his grief vividly:

> I feel these days as if some awful monster
> with a grip like a jackhammer
> has grabbed me,
> lifted me,
> shaken me,
> from head to toe, for days.
> Now that it has finally put me down, I must tread warily,
> cautiously, one foot at a time,
> watchful of the dangers
> and hurts that lurk around every corner.
> I must go gently…

The right man is the one who seizes the moment.

Goethe

GO EASY ON YOURSELF

You are not weak if you cry. You are not falling apart because you're finding it hard to get back into your old routine. You are not wallowing because you find yourself looking at photos, videos or memorabilia, or listening to songs that you liked to share. You are not going crazy because you seem forgetful or you just can't get involved in other people's small talk.

Protecting your self esteem is important right now, because grief can shatter your confidence. Don't let others label you as 'not coping', because they don't understand your way of grieving.

Do the things that nurture you. Like a walk on the beach, a hot bath, meditation, massage, afternoon naps, soothing music … try to be kind to yourself.

I will welcome happiness for it enlarges my heart; yet I will endure sadness for it opens my soul. I will acknowledge rewards for they are my due; yet I will welcome obstacles for they are my challenge.

Og Mandino

TALK ABOUT IT

This will help you to accept the truth of what's happened. It will allow the facts to 'sink in'. It will also mean you can get your feelings off your chest rather than deny or hide them. All of this is necessary ground work if you are going to get through your grief.

Friends who are good listeners, rather than ones who try to change the subject, are going to be most valuable to you right now.

Keeping a diary or just writing about the things on your mind are other useful ways of getting feelings out.

Talk to God if you feel like it – and don't be afraid to tell it like it really is for you. Your faith will not protect you from the hurt of grief, but will ultimately provide opportunities to find strength and hope to help you understand it.

Go with the pain, let it take you. Open your palms and your body to the pain. It comes in waves like the tide and you must be open as a vessel lying on the beach, letting it fill you up and then, retreating, leaving you empty and clear …

Anne Morrow Lindbergh

LOOK AFTER YOURSELF

Grief can place a real strain on your physical health. Even though you may not care about food, sleep or even how you look, it's important to give your body all the help it will need to hold you up through the tough times that could be ahead.

Remember that fresh air and gentle exercise are a better tonic for stress than alcohol or sedatives.

Releasing blocked energy, anger or frustration through active sport will not only give you the benefit of exercise, but you could find it a useful way of dealing with aggression or strong emotions.

When we avoid the legitimate suffering that results from dealing with problems, we also avoid the growth that problems demand from us.

M. Scott Peck

ASK FOR HELP

There is no reason to think that you need to cope with your grief on your own.

If you are feeling helpless or completely overwhelmed then talk to a counsellor. Ask a friend to go with you if you wish.

These days the internet is a really helpful place to find information on all aspects of loss and grief, as well as support groups and services.

Whoever thought up the sayings, 'Big boys don't cry' or 'Stand on your own two feet', probably never had to face a personal crisis themselves.

You might even find it helpful to meet other people who have been through a similar experience – you could find it a real relief to talk to someone who understands just what you're going through. Your Funeral Director will be able to tell you about bereavement support groups in your area.

If your friends offer practical help – washing the car, ironing, mowing lawns, let them do this. They need to feel they are doing something useful at a time when they feel otherwise inadequate. This is their way of saying 'I care about you'.

What lies behind us and what lies before us, are small matters compared to what lies within us.

Ralph Waldo Emerson

UNDERSTAND YOUR FRIENDS

Sometimes friends can become impatient with someone they know who is grieving. They might even say, 'You should be over it by now' or imply that there are others worse off than you.

These comments may hurt or make you angry, but your friends don't mean to do this. They are amongst a large number of people who think grief should be over in a few short weeks or months. They certainly aren't standing in your shoes and therefore they don't know about all the little reminders that seem to come out of every nook and cranny in the house.

Unfortunately, it is these friends who we turn to for support, yet what we may find is their discomfort with our presence. After the death of his wife, C. S. Lewis wrote: "I'm aware of being an embarrassment to everyone I meet ...".

When people don't know what to say to you, they may behave like this:
- Avoid mentioning the name of the person who has died
- Change the subject if you bring it up
- Talk too much about trivial things
- Avoid you – cross the street, visit less frequently
- Say things that appear thoughtless and hurtful

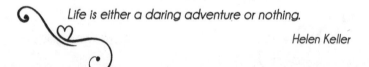

Life is either a daring adventure or nothing.

Helen Keller

LEARN TO BE ASSERTIVE

You can help your friends to know how to treat you. This will require you to tell them in plain, clear words what you need from them. Speaking up for yourself like this could mean the difference between having friends who think they are being helpful, and those who know they really are.

Using the rules of assertive communication, here is a simple three-step guide to help you get started.

Step 1 "When you ..." (explain what you don't like)
Step 2 "It's a problem because ..." (explain how you feel)
Step 3 "I'd prefer you to ..." (explain what you need)

Here's how to use it:
"When you keep telling me to give away all his things, it's a problem because I feel annoyed that you don't understand that I'm not ready to do it yet. I'd rather you didn't force me to do things, and instead just come over to keep me company."

When you learn to be assertive, you are able to tell others what you are really feeling. It helps you to ask them to try to share your grief, rather than think they have to say something to cheer you up. It shows them that one of the best ways they can help you is to let you be yourself.

Shared sorrow is half a sorrow.

Swedish Proverb

CHECK YOUR THINKING

Grief can be made worse if you pile lots of negative thoughts on top of hurt feelings. If you continually tell yourself: *'I'll never get over this'* or *'I can't live without him or her'* then you will make your road through grief even harder.

It's understandable to believe that you will never, ever survive the death of someone really special, but the other people out there in the world who have also lost a partner, parent or child are proof that you can somehow get through this. Tell yourself everyday that you are going to make it, even though it might seem impossible right now.

To give yourself encouragement, each day you could try to set a simple task to do or a goal to reach by the end of every new week – just to prove to yourself that you can make progress and that you are moving ahead.

Mostly, we can't choose how or when we're going to die; we can only choose how we're going to live. When confronted with a hopeless situation, when facing a fate that cannot be changed, we are challenged to change ourselves, especially our way of thinking.

Fear makes the wolf grow bigger.

German Proverb

BE AWARE OF ADVICE-GIVERS

Well-meaning people might make suggestions like, *'Go on a holiday'*, *'Sell the house'*, *'Have another baby'*, *'Throw away all the clothes'*, *'Keep yourself busy'*. But often advice like this is aimed at avoiding grief rather than facing it.

Comments such as these are often made by people who think that they have to say something that sounds positive, to encourage you to get on with your life.

It's wiser not to make hasty decisions or a great number of extra changes in your routine right now. Nor will a new house, new baby or new job erase your grief or replace a person who has died.

Let us be grateful for people who make us happy. They are the charming gardeners who make our souls blossom.

Marcel Proust

BE PREPARED FOR UPS AND DOWNS

Grief is rarely a smooth road to travel. Some people expect themselves 'to be over it' or 'be back to my old self again' in a short space of time. Then, they are surprised to be tripped up by memories when a birthday or anniversary comes along. These times of the year can cause a return of very intense feelings and the lead up can be like a dreaded countdown as you remember the way things were last year, last Christmas, last birthday – when your loved one was still here.

Spend such days however you wish. A visit to the cemetery might be a natural thing to do for some people but not for others. You might like to create your own special ritual of remembrance – a lighted candle on the Christmas table, a quiet get together with some special friends, a gift to a favourite charity 'In memory of ...'.

The important thing to remember is to acknowledge how you feel on these days – putting on a brave face might just be too hard. Let your family and friends know how you would prefer to spend the time – do you want to change the venue for Christmas dinner? How do you feel about sending Christmas cards this year? Would you like some visitors over for a birthday or anniversary remembrance or would you prefer a quiet day at home?

What would you attempt to do,
if you knew you could not fail?

Dr Robert Schuller

KNOW THERE WILL BE MEMORY TRIGGERS
ALL AROUND YOU

It may not even be a significant event that causes a set back. A flood of tears might happen when you least expect it. Seeing other families spending time with each other. Driving past a familiar place you enjoyed together. It could be hearing a favourite song on the radio. For bereaved parents it might be seeing a child the same age as their own who died. It could be the sight of a car like your loved one drove. Or even a similar hairdo or item of clothing which jumps out at you in a crowd. It could be the smell of perfume or aftershave. Anything.

Any little reminder could set off tears or another 'bad day'.

You don't need to explain why you are upset, nor do you need to apologise if others feel uncomfortable around you. Just as you are learning to make readjustments in your life, your friends will also have to learn about grief and how it is affecting you ... and them.

The true way to mourn the dead is to take care of the living who belong to them.

Edmund Burke

HAVE THE COURAGE TO DO THE HARD THINGS

There will be many personal possessions which you will need to sort through – some will not be practical to keep, others will be treasured forever. This can be such an emotional dilemma. It's one of the hard things you're going to have to do.

At first, you might move through guilty thoughts – *Will it seem like I'm throwing him out? Does it mean I no longer love her? Am I trying to push him out of my life? Is it too soon to be making these changes? Should I leave everything as is?*

Things like a stamp collection, golf clubs, recipe books, tools, knitting needles … these may have been a favourite part of your loved one's lifestyle, but you don't have to keep them if they are of no use to you. When you make the decision to finally 'let go' of something, you can be left with a feeling of relief and possibly even freedom. And don't be surprised if you get sentimental over the most trivial things.

Timing is important. Don't part with anything until you can do so comfortably. It doesn't mean that selling the family car or packing away toys and teddy bears won't hurt. It just means you are doing it because you are ready to do so.

Ever had a memory that sneaks out of your eye and rolls down your cheek?

Unknown

CONTINUE THE BOND

Here is an idea that's borne from the experiences of grieving people. They want to maintain a connection with the person who has died. They want to acknowledge the bond that was there. They don't want to act like they never existed.

They find it comforting when they can remember them in fitting ways and show how much they meant. Here are some examples:
- Celebrate them on their birthday
- Create an annual family day around their hobby – a golf day, a BBQ, a movie night
- At special times of the year, play their favourite music, cook their favourite meal
- Raise a glass and toast them whenever the family gets together
- Wear an item of their jewellery
- Keep their name alive in conversations

These connections may change over time and as circumstances alter, but they are important ways of saying "we remember you", alongside the knowledge that a new life has to be built without this person.

See. I will not forget you.
I have carved you on the palms of my hands.

Isaiah 49:16

ACCEPT LOSS AS A PART OF LIFE

Yes, whether we like it or not, loss in its many forms cannot be avoided. Whilst we all know that death is a natural part of living, when it happens to someone we know, we are often shocked and believe it's unfair. We may ask 'why?' over and over. But we have to face the reality that bad things do happen to good people.

But grief is a teacher – through loss we can grow in courage and wisdom and learn to appreciate the pain and loneliness of others. It also presents an opportunity to develop our values, beliefs and relationships as we work out just who and what really matter in our lives. Yet, it's a hard way to learn. We may not like it. It can be a frightening and lonely experience. But if we choose to love someone, we must also be willing to let that person go when their life comes to an end.

If you understand, things are just as they are.
If you do not understand, things are just as they are.

Zen Koan

CHAPTER 4

IF YOU KNOW SOMEONE WHO IS GRIEVING

Many people find it hard to approach or talk to someone they know who is grieving. Should you bring up the subject first? What if you upset them? Should you mind your own business? What if they start to cry?

It is an accepted fact that grieving people receive most of their support immediately after the death and in the following weeks. But, as time goes by, reluctance, silence and avoidance become the norm for their friends. Not because they choose to be evasive or unkind, but rather because they don't know what to say.

Arm yourself with empathy – these are words that you choose when you respond to your friend to show you accept that their grief is what they say it is and you understand why they are feeling that way. This also stops those one-line clichés from slipping out – *God's will. You'll be okay. Be brave. It could have been worse.* Comments like these usually have very little connection to the way a grieving person feels and add to their hurt and sense of isolation.

There is a time to keep silent and a time to speak.

Ecclesiastes

THERE WILL BE EXPECTATIONS

When you are grieving, you do expect some kind of acknowledgement that you have been through a difficult experience. Friends may disappoint, and add to the sense of loss, when they don't know how to make an approach.

"No-one would talk to me about her. They had this wrong idea they would upset me ... they just couldn't handle it ... they changed the subject, looked at their feet, looked at the ceiling."

Don, bereaved father of a teenage daughter

"'Oh you're so strong, you'll be okay.' What is that supposed to mean? That I shouldn't feel suicidal, shredded, insane, lost, lonely ... Three different people said that to me, it really mystified me and hurt me."

Jill, widow of Paul

"I need to be listened to, to know that I'm okay. They all think that I'm over it but this clever charade is only because I've found so few people able to listen."

Rebecca, fiancée of motor accident victim

*We are healed from suffering only
by experiencing it to the full.*

Marcel Proust

ASK HOW THINGS ARE GOING

A word of caution first. If you ask a grieving person, "How are you?", it's just as easy for them to reply, "Fine thanks". We all do it, often just through habit.

If you want to show that you genuinely want to know how things are, you will need to ask in such a way that your intentions are clear:

- How are things at home these days?
- How are you managing on your own?
- How is everyone in the family doing?

Sometimes, grieving people will need more encouragement to know that it is alright to talk about what's happened and how they're coping. So you may need to say something specific like this:

- You always tell me you're fine, but are you really okay?
- I know you said you're fine, but you look a bit down.
- You tell us you're alright but I'm not so sure. We never see you around anymore.

Great works are performed, not by strength, but by perseverance.

Samuel Johnson

YOU DON'T HAVE TO FIX IT

Try not to make statements that encourage grieving people to keep their grief silent and locked inside themselves.

Be brave.
Take it like a man.
Crying won't change a thing.
Put it behind you and get on with your life.
Don't talk about it, you'll just upset yourself.

Instead, give permission for their grief to be expressed. You don't have to fix it or cheer them up. You just need to have the courage to stay and listen.

You help by listening because you show you are not embarrassed or awkward about someone else's feelings. You also give the message that grief does not have to be an isolating experience. By inviting them to talk freely if they wish, you provide an opportunity for them to review the relationship, the circumstances of the death, what they're worried about or anything else that matters most right now.

This kind of communication assists grieving people to deal with the reality of someone's death and the changes that result. Your role is to show you accept and understand what they're going through – this is empathy.

I never take counsel of my fears.

Gen. George Patton

WAIT IN SUSPENSE

The word 'listen' has ancient Anglo Saxon origins: *hylstan* which means 'learning', and *hlosnian* - 'to wait in suspense'.

If we combine the idea of waiting in suspense in order to learn about our friend's grief, we have a good starting point for our role as a helpful listener.

This is a different approach from someone who says, *"I know how you feel"*. When grieving people hear this remark, there is no incentive to tell you how they are feeling. In fact, it often sparks hostility and resentment as they are left wondering how anyone could possibly know what their own unique pain feels like.

However, when you have learned something of your friend's grief, you may be able to reply with empathy, *"I understand what you're feeling. I see what you mean."*

You listen with only one purpose: to help him or her to empty his heart. You just listen with compassion and help him to suffer less.

Thich Nhat Hanh

IF THEY START TO CRY

There's no need to say something to stop the tears like:
- *Don't cry. He wouldn't want you to get so upset.*
- *Dry your eyes and we'll talk about something else.*
- *It's no use crying over spilt milk.*

Instead, try saying something like:
- *It's alright to cry.*
- *Don't worry about crying, that's one way to get it all off your chest.*
- *I can see how much you miss her. No wonder you're sad.*

Crying helps emotions to be released. The idea of 'being strong' works directly against this principle. Often we would prefer people not to cry in front of us because it makes us feel uneasy or upset. Why not tell your friend that you're not sure what to do when they're upset. You might find they expect no more than your presence beside them. Words may be unnecessary.

The road to the heart is the ear.

Voltaire

WHY DID THIS HAPPEN TO ME?

'Why?' is almost a universal question asked by grieving people. *Why did this happen to our family? Why did God let this happen? Why someone so young?*

When these questions are directed at you, fortunately you don't need to struggle to find an answer. Just let the questions be asked. Rarely, does the response, 'It's God's will' stop the questioning either.

Grief work involves a search for meaning, a need to make sense of the events surrounding the death. Gradually, a point of understanding can be reached. Answers will surface – even if the answer is, 'there is no answer'.

Assure your friend that this questioning is a normal part of their grief:
- *I can see how hard it is to rest easy when you can't understand why it happened.*
- *It sounds like nothing makes sense to you and you feel like you're going crazy.*
- *No wonder you can't sleep with all those nagging questions going around in your head.*

Things do not change. We change.

Henry David Thoreau

BE READY FOR ANGER

Being angry is a common part of grief. But it can be very difficult to deal with another person's anger. We don't need to snap them out of it or urge them to suppress it.

A helpful approach is to acknowledge it, so that it can be shared, vented and let go.

Avoid saying:
- *Don't talk like that.*
- *Try to think of all the good times instead.*
- *There are others worse off than you.*

Instead, try empathetic words like:
- *It must be hard to accept that something like this could happen to you.*
- *It does seem unfair, no wonder it makes you angry.*
- *I can sense you're mad at the world because your whole life has changed.*

Goodness is not gone from the world because one good person has died.
Meaning is not gone from this life because one who meant so much is no longer present.

Colin Murray Parkes

ALLOW GUILT TO BE EXPRESSED

To hear a grieving person review their regrets or confide their guilt with you can be frightening. Their thoughts may not even be logical, especially when we know how their desire to turn back the clock is impossible.

- *If only I'd said sorry after that fight we had.*
- *I wish I'd paid more attention when he said he was so depressed.*
- *I should have gone to the hospital more often to see her.*

Again, your role is to allow even these painful thoughts to be shared. You don't need to come up with a solution to their problem. Nor should you encourage them to stifle such strong feelings, or criticise them for having such thoughts.

Instead, show you understand by saying:

- *There are so many doubts and loose ends. It must be hard for you to make sense of it all.*
- *You feel responsible in some way. I guess it will take a long time to sort it all out.*
- *It sounds like there are lots of things you never got a chance to say. What would you like to say to him right now?*

What wound did ever heal but by degrees?

Shakespeare, Othello

VALUE THE DIFFERENCE

It's wise to remind yourself that you cannot predict how a grieving person will behave – even your best friend or a family member. There are so many individual factors to consider.

Some might not want to talk about it, despite your best efforts at listening. Privacy might be all they ask from those around them.

Some might be relieved that a long illness is finally over, whilst the impending loss provided opportunities to mend old wounds or be there right to the end. A pervasive peace might be more evident than distress and sorrow.

Some are strengthened by their faith, knowing that to be with God means to be free from the troubles of our earthly lives. Hope comes from the promise of eternal life and being reunited with loved ones.

Others may avoid all attempts to be helped or seek help. It's just too painful. It's easier to try to forget rather than learn to cope with the memories, the changes, the reality.

We don't make mistakes.
We just have learnings.

Anne Wilson Schaef

STAY IN TOUCH

Remember that grief doesn't go away in a few short weeks. Even one or two or more years might not be long enough to adjust to the changes that have to be made.

Sometimes it's easy to say, *"Give me a call if there's anything I can do."* Yet, grieving people often don't want to be a nuisance, or possibly their pride prevents them from asking for a hand with household chores or legal matters or financial problems.

So, a friend who calls in three, six or twelve months time might be one of the few who still asks how things are going.

A friend who mentions the name of the person who has died might be one of the few who invites a conversation about old times and other memories.

A friend who remembers special days like birthdays or a first Christmas on your own, might be one of the few who has picked up the phone to say, *"I was thinking of you today."*

We do not have to rely on memories to recapture the
spirit of those we have loved and lost –
they live within our souls in some perfect sanctuary
which even death cannot destroy.

Nan Witcomb

ON SETTING FORTH

May the road rise to meet you.
May the wind always be at your back.
May the sun shine warm upon your face.
The rain fall soft upon your fields;
And, until we meet again, may
God hold you in the palm of his hand.

Traditional Celtic Blessing

As you set forth, you might find it helpful to record your own observations, reflections, tips and reminders of the pitfalls and the progress as you make your way through the maze of grief.

....

....

....

....

....

....

....

....

....

....

....

....

....

....

....

....

....

....

....

....

....

....

....

....

....

....

....

....

....

....

....

....

....

....

....

....

....

....